WorkMatters®

ISBN-978-0-9789678-5-7

WorkMatters, Inc.

P.O. Box 130756
Birmingham, AL 35213 USA

205-879-8494
gayle@workmatters.com
WorkMatters.com

I'm so glad you have a copy of the Life Work Planning Workbook.

To download a free copy of:

My List of Best Life Work Planning Tips & Common Mistakes to Avoid,

please send an email to:

LifeWorkTips@workmatters.com

We'll send it to you right away!

And we can notify you of upcoming Life Work Planning Retreats and other events that may be of interest.

Wishing you the best as you pursue what's most important in your life and work.

Gayle

About Gayle Lantz

Gayle Lantz is a leadership expert and founder of WorkMatters, Inc. (www.WorkMatters.com), a consulting firm dedicated to helping leaders think and work smarter.

A sought-after consultant, executive coach, facilitator, and speaker, Gayle works closely with executives and leadership teams to expand their vision, think and act strategically, and inspire change. Together, they increase business results and help make work matter at every level of the organization. Among her clients are NASA, Microsoft, MassMutual, Southern Company, Lockheed Martin, BBVA Compass Bank as well as a variety of small and mid-sized professional service firms.

Gayle runs senior executive roundtable groups with executives from non-competing industries. Participants meet regularly to exchange ideas, sharpen executive leadership skills, and gain objective perspective to help them grow their business.

Gayle authored the award-winning book *Take the Bull by the Horns: The Busy Leader's Action Guide to Growing Your Business...and Yourself.* She has also created *The Leadership Journal* and *My Daily Coach* app.

Before starting her own business, Gayle worked as an executive in the insurance, financial services, and investment industry. She most recently held an officer position with TIAA-CREF—an industry leader serving people in the academic, medical, cultural, and research fields.

Gayle's articles and/or quotations have been featured in a variety of national and global business publications including *BusinessWeek, Harvard Management Update, Wall Street Journal Online, FastCompany.com, CEO Online,* and *The New York Times.*

A graduate of Emory University in Atlanta, Georgia, Gayle lives in Birmingham, Alabama, and has been honored as one of Birmingham's Top 10 Women in Business.

TABLE OF CONTENTS

INTRODUCTION

Where do you start?
What should you consider?
How do you know if you're on the right path?

Whenever you're trying to "figure out" what's next for you, the process can seem overwhelming.

These are common questions that come up frequently in my work with executives and other professionals.

For many years in my consulting and coaching work, I've seen executive clients who are so busy running their businesses that they've lost sight of *themselves*—who they are and what they really want.

They've been successful in their roles, but they sense something is missing or they're burning themselves out.

Their lives are being run by their calendars, their assistants, or people other than themselves.

This Workbook is for you if:

You want to make improvements in your life or your work.

You have reached a turning point (or anticipate being there soon) in your life, work, role, or business.

You are open to the idea of reinvention.

You simply want to re-energize yourself.

You feel tired of living your life by default or feeling like you're stuck on autopilot.

You've recently experienced a major event in your personal life—marriage, divorce, loss of a loved one, personal crisis, new baby, empty nesting, to name a few possibilities.

Perhaps you've recently experienced a major event in your work—a promotion, new role, new business, merger, layoff, new project, and more.

Or you've simply been "too busy" to truly focus on YOU.

It's my hope that using this Life Work Planning Workbook allows you to be more deliberate about creating what you *really* want in your life and work—and enjoying the process, too.

A Note About Life Work Planning

The term "Life Work Planning" was introduced to me by Richard N. Bolles, author of the classic best-selling career book, *What Color is Your Parachute?*

I attended the author's Life Work Planning Retreat years ago in Bend, Oregon. The retreat was one of the most impactful experiences of my life. In contemplating my own life's work, I discovered my desire (and now commitment) to help others get what they want in their life and work.

After the retreat, I represented Bolles's work as I started my new consulting/coaching business. This step allowed me to serve people worldwide who were planning careers they really wanted.

As Bolles explained, we all do life work planning activities in some form every day. He said, "The **discipline** called Life Work Planning is only a more systematic, thoughtful, and thorough way of doing something you already do occasionally, intuitively, and without much agonizing thought."

Life Work Planning is often associated with job hunting; however, many of the same principles and processes in Life Work Planning can be applied in a business context. I have successfully adapted these principles to help clients improve themselves, their teams, and their businesses. The process involves gaining clarity and a little strategic thinking.

In the Life Work Planning process, as in strategic planning, you'll find the most value in the *process itself*—in the conversations you have with yourself or others, the kinds of ideas you're considering, and the clarity you're gaining. It includes the decisions you'll make about what you say "yes" or "no" to.

The plan itself may be nice to have, but know that it will change. However, the **discipline** of Life Work Planning is a unique skill you can carry with you. It will serve you over and over as you determine what's next for you at any point in your life.

Learning to think deliberately and honestly about what you really want prepares you for each new growth opportunity. It keeps you in the driver's seat.

Work is a part of life.

For purposes of the Workbook, you might consider "life" to represent personal or family matters, while "work" represents your job, profession, position, livelihood, or business.

Yes, work is a part of life—the **one life** you have. Still, it's helpful to look at each element separately while acknowledging that one influences the other.

Companies Are Getting It

It's good to see that companies are recognizing the importance of holistic approaches to help employees be productive, develop skills, and create experiences that help them in both work and life.

The companies that get it are considering the whole person in their hiring, development, and retention efforts.

There's no denying what happens in your personal life affects your work life and vice versa.

Don't you want to bring your **whole self** to work and not feel like you're leaving parts of yourself behind?

The best leaders understand the potential they have to positively impact a person as a human being, not just the bottom line.

About this Life Work Planning Workbook

This Workbook helps you focus on areas that are most important to consider as you contemplate your future.

Ideally, it was created as a resource for participants in my Life Work Planning Retreats, but you can use it on your own as well. You'll find ample space to capture notes as you go along. **Writing or journaling** about these ideas is one way to ensure they become tangible.

What I've seen with other people and experienced myself is this: *You might work too hard on figuring things out!* The process doesn't have to be arduous, especially if you involve people like you who want to make the most of their lives and work. It can actually be fun and energizing.

The irony is that if you can simply relax into the process and trust your instincts, better ideas will come. Instead of working hard to find the ideal path, you'll discover that *the path actually finds you!*

Think of this as a Life Work Planning Chillbook as opposed to a Workbook.

We won't necessarily take a linear path to our planning process, but let's make it as simple as possible by organizing the ideas in a framework of elements that work together synergistically. For example, you might do work in one area that makes you change, improve, or clarify work you've done in another area.

Here's the basic model:

LIFE WORK PLANNING

VISION
FUTURE STATE

MINDSET
INNER STATE

ACTION
CURRENT STATE

YOUR
BEST SELF

SUPPORT

YOUR FUTURE STATE

VISION

Interests · Role · Values · Impact · Skills · People · Strengths

Where are you going?

What does the picture look like?

VISION

A natural starting point to the process is to ask, "Where do you want to go?" This question is logical, but you may have difficulty answering it. You may only know you don't want to be where you are now.

If you feel like you're on a merry-go-round without time to even think, you'll simply have to jump off and get your bearings. Spend time away from your normal routine so you can think differently. Quiet your mind and begin imagining new possibilities.

When I ask people what vision they have for themselves, I've seen three basic patterns emerge:

1. **Default:** Some people describe a version of their future that's somewhat like they're experiencing now. Operating on autopilot, they haven't given a lot of thought to what's next. They're trying to keep up with the day-to-day grind with a tendency to look at today only.

2. **Fuzzy:** These people have a general idea about what they want to be better or different, but the picture isn't clear. They can anticipate that changes are coming, but they don't know how they will deal with them.

3. **Clear:** These people can describe in specific detail what they want to see happen. In many ways, that helps them be more deliberate about moving toward that vision. On the other hand, if their vision is too set, opportunities could be missed or they could be setting themselves up for disappointment.

Where do you get stuck?

Describe your vision of how you see yourself in the future (in your life, work, or business). If you're like most people, you probably need to develop more clarity.

If you get stuck creating a vision, these techniques can help you get your juices flowing:

- Describe your vision as though you're describing a movie scene. Where are you two or three years from now? What's happening in the scene? Who are the people in your vision? Where are you? What's your role? What are you doing? How are you feeling? Capture the idea, image, and/or feeling to represent what you *really* want— not what you think you should want.

12

- Write a letter to a loved one as though it's three years from now. Describe key highlights about what you've done and ideally what you're experiencing three years from now. Include something you're most proud of or grateful for. You might start your letter by saying, "Dear _____, I'm so happy because . . ." or "I love what I'm doing now because . . ." or "I'm thriving in my business because . . ."

- Reflect on your childhood for a moment. What were the dreams and hopes you had as a child? Don't dismiss them; they often hold clues about what you want in your future.

- Recall various points of your past that were among your best moments—experiences that represent a specific challenge you worked through or a time when you were especially proud of something you accomplished. Perhaps describe a time when you felt "in the flow." *

*See STORIES EXERCISE on p.37. Immediately after you complete it, do the PRIORITIZING EXERCISE.

- Just start writing. Free flow. Don't overthink. Trust your instincts. See what ideas come up. If needed, force yourself to write for five or 10 minutes straight without stopping or editing. (After all, you're the only one reading the piece you write ☺.)

MY VISION:

_____
_____
_____
_____
_____
_____
_____
_____
_____
_____
_____
_____
_____
_____
_____
_____
_____
_____
_____
_____
_____
_____
_____
_____
_____
_____
_____
_____
_____
_____

MY VISION (continued):

_____
_____
_____
_____
_____
_____
_____
_____
_____
_____
_____
_____
_____
_____
_____
_____
_____
_____
_____
_____
_____
_____
_____
_____
_____
_____
_____
_____
_____
_____
_____
_____
_____

MY VISION (continued):

_____
_____
_____
_____
_____
_____
_____
_____
_____
_____
_____
_____
_____
_____
_____
_____
_____
_____
_____
_____
_____
_____
_____
_____
_____
_____
_____
_____
_____
_____
_____
_____
_____
_____
_____
_____
_____
_____

YOUR INNER STATE

MINDSET

Feelings

Beliefs

Attitude

Mentality

Emotions

Thoughts

What are you thinking?

What are you feeling?

MINDSET

Now that you've captured a form of your vision on paper, the voices in your head might sound something like this:

Well, that would be nice, but it probably won't happen.

That would be crazy if it really happened.

What was I thinking?

What will people think?

I've got to be more realistic . . .

The vision you created reveals what you *really* want, so keep your focus on it.

But don't start developing a plan to achieve your exact vision yet. It's premature to do that, especially if deep down you hold beliefs that prevent you from making it happen.

The key is aligning your beliefs to match your vision. This takes practice. (I'm not referring to religious beliefs here, although your religious beliefs may be a positive or negative influence on your overall beliefs.)

Think of your beliefs as *ideas you consider to be true*.

Don't judge a belief as good or bad; simply note if you think it's a belief that hinders you or empowers you.

BELIEFS EXERCISE

1. On page 20, randomly list all the reasons you think you can't achieve what you want. That usually comes naturally. It's easy to sabotage yourself with thoughts such as, "I'm not smart enough. I don't have the energy. I can't do this alone. No one will support me, etc."

Make this list to get it out of your system. Do a brain dump quickly. Don't overthink it.

18

2. Then on page 21, write beliefs that you could give you more power and momentum. That includes thoughts such as "I'm smart enough to figure things out. I'm building or regaining my energy. I will find the support I need."

It's important you don't write statements of belief you think you SHOULD hold. Instead, your job is to write statements that you **could potentially believe**. Move quickly to get the ideas flowing.

3. List those beliefs you need to get rid of or change in the section provided on page 22.

4. Then list those NEW beliefs you could hold on page 23. If a belief seems too extreme or outrageous to you, make it more general. For example, if it feels too crazy to believe "I'll make a million dollars this year," then write a less specific statement such as "I'll make the money I need this year to do what I want." Typically, it's easier to internalize more general statements.

Capture your beliefs about yourself as well as your beliefs about other people or situations.

Some beliefs you're not even aware of; they're hidden. You may have tuned them *out* like background music. Now is the time to tune *in* to your beliefs.

Keep in mind that beliefs you've held for a long time are the most difficult to change. You can't flip a switch, but you can begin "trying on" new beliefs and see how they feel.

For many years, I didn't believe I could speak in public. I told myself, "I'll pass out. I'll forget what I'm trying to say . . ." My anxiety was overwhelming. But then I shifted my thinking to: "I think I can get through a talk." From there, I shifted my belief to: "I think I can give a unique presentation that will have a positive impact."

As a naturally private person, I've had to shift my beliefs about increasing my visibility and expressing myself more publicly. I'm increasingly motivated to do that because I believe it will help me reach more people so I can help make a difference in their lives.

Your beliefs shape your mindset.

How set is *your* mind? Do you think you can develop the mindset you need to achieve what you want?

To find out, do the BELIEFS EXERCISE on the pages that follow.

"Whether you think you can or you think you can't, you're right." ~ Henry Ford

NEGATIVE BELIEFS THAT HOLD ME BACK:

_____
_____
_____
_____
_____
_____
_____
_____
_____
_____
_____
_____
_____
_____
_____
_____
_____
_____
_____
_____
_____
_____
_____
_____
_____
_____
_____
_____
_____
_____

POSITIVE BELIEFS THAT GIVE ME STRENGTH & POWER:

_____

_____

_____

_____

_____

_____

_____

_____

_____

_____

_____

_____

_____

_____

_____

_____

_____

_____

_____

_____

_____

_____

_____

_____

_____

_____

_____

_____

_____

_____

_____

_____

NEGATIVE BELIEFS I NEED TO LET GO OF OR REPLACE:

_____

_____

_____

_____

_____

_____

_____

_____

_____

_____

_____

_____

_____

_____

_____

_____

_____

_____

_____

_____

_____

_____

_____

_____

_____

_____

_____

_____

_____

_____

_____

_____

NEW POSITIVE BELIEFS I CAN HOLD:

_____
_____
_____
_____
_____
_____
_____
_____
_____
_____
_____
_____
_____
_____
_____
_____
_____
_____
_____
_____
_____
_____
_____
_____
_____
_____
_____
_____
_____
_____

You might put a bookmark on this **BELIEFS EXERCISE** so you can return to it easily throughout this experience. Your beliefs can be challenged, clarified, strengthened, and even changed over time.

Combining VISION and MINDSET

"Most of us have two lives. The life we live, and the unlived life within us.
Between the two stands Resistance." ~ Steven Pressfield

Ready to move forward? Release the resistance. Keep your focus on your vision.

It's like exercising a muscle you don't use often. It's simply easier to look back at your past or to look at where you are now.

Instead, practice allowing yourself to live in your BEST future. How? By describing your best future in *present tense*, as though it's happening now.

For example, instead of saying, "I want to expand my influence," say, "I'm expanding my influence." Seems like a subtle shift, but it can help strengthen your mindset and energy to achieve what you want.

Let's see if your mindset supports your vision.

Sometimes it might take quite a while to line up your thinking with the vision you have for your life and work. It's likely easier to talk yourself out of going for what you really want. That's resistance kicking in.

You must find ways to talk yourself *into* what you really want.

Revisit the vision you created in an earlier exercise. How excited are you about it on a scale of 1-10? (1 is "not much" and 10 is "super excited.")

Refine your vision until it at least reflects a "9" on your scale. Make it as compelling as possible and don't let your "realistic" voice stop you.

Ideally, you'll create a vision for your life, work, or business that you feel you can't *not* do. (In fact, that's part of what compelled me to create this content and run Life Work Planning Retreats. After thinking about it for a long time, I finally got to a point where I said, "I just have to do this!" The timing felt right.)

The same goes in business. Leaders in the best companies have big, bold visions. It takes time to get employees on board with their visions because they're stuck in old patterns of thinking. You might be stuck in similar ways that hold you back. (More on that later.)

For now, let's focus on key mindset factors to consider in this process:
1. Identity
2. Assessment

IDENTITY: Who are you?

"I don't want other people to decide who I am. I want to decide that for myself."
~ Emma Watson

Your self-identity is one of the most important factors that will affect your success. It's important to take a close look at how your identity has been shaped and how you can adapt it as needed.

We all go through similar phases of identifying ourselves as a child, teenager, adult, etc. Our identities are mostly shaped by our families, our faiths, and our communities. But other parts are shaped by our work, our professions, or our businesses.

When I left my corporate job and started my own business, I went through an adjustment in identity. It took me a few years to settle into the idea that I'm an entrepreneur (especially after being in corporate management for so long). I have taken on multiple identities since then.

I learned that *how I view myself* is more important than how others view me.

For example, it doesn't matter if someone knows me as a consultant, coach, speaker, writer, facilitator. I just see myself as a versatile resource—an expert in my field who serves my market in a variety of ways.

Apart from professional labels, what descriptors come to mind when you consider how you see yourself?

Are they words that give you strength?
e.g., Strong, Valuable, Fearless, Abundant, etc.

OR

Are they words that diminish you?
Weak, Unworthy, Fearful, Lacking, etc.

Become more aware of how you think about yourself.

Lose the many layers

Some clients admit they're not sure who they are anymore. If you're like them, over the years you keep adding new layers of identity—like a Russian doll. You fit yourself into a new shell.

As you take on new roles, sometimes you feel like you have to become a little bigger, better, or different.

As the doll keeps getting bigger, sometimes it's hard to find the smallest doll inside. The solid one. The one that represents your core.

It's there.

You must reconnect with your core to do your best Life Work Planning.

Be congruent

Do you have a longing for integration of your personal self and your work self?

You may be drawn to Life Work Planning now because you sense an incongruence between *who you are* and *what you think you're supposed to do*. That's why you start by understanding yourself first.

It's likely you've tried to force fit yourself into a role or opportunity that doesn't feel right today. Or worse, you've convinced yourself you *are* your outer shell.

Now is the time to reclaim your true identity.

"Be yourself" sounds like trite advice, but it takes on new meaning as an adult. You can do your best life's work when you can be unapologetically *you*.

If you're in a leadership role, don't be afraid to bring more of your true self and your unique natural strengths to your role.

Words of wisdom from poet, David Whyte:

> *"We are each a river with a particular abiding character, but we show radically different aspects of our self according to the territory through which we travel."*

What identity do you see for yourself in the future?

Begin adjusting to it. This might take time, but it's worth it.

AGE SEVEN:

Some experts argue that your identity is established at a very early age.

One of the most fascinating documentaries I saw focused on this issue is *Seven Up*—a British documentary originally filmed in 1964. It's since been developed into the *Up* series on TV.

As described on Amazon.com: "The premise behind the *Up* series is deceptively simple: take a cross-section of children at age seven, ask them about their hopes for the future, and then return every seven years to mark their progress."

Can you imagine being interviewed every seven years over the past five decades? Many of these kids are now grandparents. It's interesting to see the patterns that continue over so many years. And, in some cases, wishes that came true.

For example, the young boy living in an orphanage-like setting longed for family. As an adult, he became a foster parent and had a family of his own.

Now think about the person you were at age seven. What were your hopes and aspirations then?

The *Up* series is a reminder of how fleeting life is. That's more reason to be involved in THIS process—to figure out what you *really* want and make it happen now!

ASSESSMENTS

Chances are you've had the opportunity to take an assessment or two in your life, especially if you've worked in the corporate world.

Assessments can be used for a variety of purposes, and different ones are available in the marketplace. They help you see yourself more clearly in specific areas of life and work.

Some measure personality type, behavioral style, motivational factors, skills, emotional intelligence, leadership style, strengths, and other areas.

If you haven't taken an assessment in a while, do so because . . .

a) You'll likely discover something new about yourself that you hadn't realized.
b) You'll likely validate something about you that's good to know.

Ask your employer about any assessments they offer. Or do some research on your own.

Feel free to contact me to determine which assessments I offer that could be helpful to you.

Initially, I was skeptical about assessments, thinking they pigeonhole or label a person. However, my experience taught me that, when debriefed properly, they can be extremely valuable. That's why I offer different types of assessments to help guide my clients (both individuals and organizations) in a variety of areas.

One assessment I took years ago told me my type was "Trailblazer"—a new concept as it applied to me. Yet knowing this helped me step into my entrepreneurial role with more confidence.

Determine if or when you'd like to take an assessment as part of your Life Work Planning process. Doing so helps you answer the "Who are you?" question.

The better you know yourself, the better chance you have of creating what you really want.

30

YOUR CURRENT STATE

ACTION

Motivated

"Busy"

Inspired

Strategic

Reactive

Impulsive

What are you doing now?

Why are you doing it now?

ACTION

Now what?

By now, I hope you have more clarity about what you'd like to see in the future—in your life and work. Keep refining your vision as you need to.

Here's something that often trips people up—that is, believing you have to know exactly what you want before you take action.

The truth is this: More clarity will come as you take *some* action. You don't have to do anything radical, but you do need to stay in motion.

As you take a few small steps in one direction, they will likely open new possibilities. They could also show you more of what you want or *don't* want. Either way, you're making progress.

You can't redirect yourself unless you're in motion.

Ask yourself, "What could I be doing now? What should I be doing now?"

When you're focused on action, consider these questions:

- Is what you're doing now helping you move forward in the way you want?
  If so, congrats. Keep it up!

- If not, what can you do now to help you move forward in the way you want (something immediate or short term)?

What action do you want to take in the future to help you move forward?

PLANNING

When I'm doing strategic planning with businesses, people like to focus on the actual plan first.
They want something clear and tangible—a blueprint, a map they can follow step by step.

It's similar in Life Work Planning. You want to first know *what the path is* and *what steps to take immediately.*

However, if you haven't done the right thinking on the front end to assess *who you are* and *what you really want,* creating a plan is useless.

It's not difficult to put together a plan that seems logical because it's usually an extension of where you are now. It's more challenging to rethink the big picture and consider completely new possibilities that are exciting and compelling.

And the toughest part is not necessarily conjuring up the ideas; it's BELIEVING you can make them happen.

You can make them happen.

"Life is what happens to us while we are making other plans." ~ *Allen Saunders*

How to think about your plan

Instead of thinking about your plan as a step-by-step time-and-action map, think of it as a guide—one that helps you set direction, make decisions, and establish better boundaries.

The trick is remaining calm and carrying on as you adjust and move forward. That's why a significant portion of my Life Work Planning approach is devoted to mindset.

Of course, your plan will need to be reviewed, updated, and modified as needed. Too many people feel discouraged when their plan changes or something unexpected derails it. That's normal.

People fool themselves into thinking the plan is the most important part. Instead, what's most important is how you FEEL and THINK about everything as you work your plan. If it doesn't feel right, be willing to make needed changes.

As you're designing your plan, keep it simple. You might establish three key goals for yourself that include milestones or measures of success. Or you might simply create a vision board with pictures, words, ideas, or concepts that keep your future desired state in view.

Depending on your goals, you might need a general long-term plan (e.g., what you'll accomplish over the next five years) or a specific short-term plan (e.g., what you'll accomplish over the next 90 days).

Keep your plan outcome-oriented. To do that, ask questions like:

What is the result I want to achieve? By when?

What is the impact I want to make? By when?

What will I have accomplished? By when?

Some people develop project-focused plans and call what they're trying to accomplish a "project." This approach is common in business, and it can work in personal planning as well.

Whatever form or template you prefer, do write down your plan. That way, it will be "real" and more likely to get done.

Whether you prefer a structured way to take action or you operate more intuitively, do what works for you. There's no step-by-step formula that's right for everyone.

Notes: Use these pages to capture three main goals or outcomes related to your life or work. Include milestones or measures of success.

_____
_____
_____
_____
_____
_____
_____
_____
_____
_____
_____
_____
_____
_____
_____
_____
_____
_____
_____
_____
_____
_____
_____
_____
_____
_____
_____
_____
_____
_____
_____
_____

Notes (continued):

_____

_____

_____

_____

_____

_____

_____

_____

_____

_____

_____

_____

_____

_____

_____

_____

_____

_____

_____

_____

_____

_____

_____

_____

_____

_____

_____

_____

_____

_____

_____

_____

_____

_____

_____

YOUR FOUNDATION

SUPPORT

PEOPLE	ENVIRONMENT
Advocates	Community
Peers Mentors	Home Office
Team Members	Inspirational
Friends	Health Learning
Family	Emotional

In what specific areas do you need more support?

What could be possible for you if you have all the support you need?

SUPPORT

Get the support you need in your life to work on all three areas: vision, mindset, and action.

At times, you need help expanding possibilities for yourself or your business. At other times, you need to strengthen your own mindset. And there are times when you need help taking action.

Think of building support in two main areas: People and Environment

PEOPLE:

You can't underestimate the importance of building a substantial support network. If you're lucky, some people will support you in both your personal and professional life.

You are not alone. But it might feel like it if . . .

a) You are growing and other people (family, friends, colleagues) are not growing at the same pace.
b) Your experience seems different from others you know. It's hard to find people who can relate to you.
c) You've been through challenging personal situations that affect your personal or professional network.

Seek out:

- Advocates
- Mentors/Coaches
- Peers/Colleagues
- Family members/Friends
- Role Models

ENVIRONMENT:

Your environmental support includes:

- Geographic/Physical
- Spiritual/Inspirational
- Intellectual/Learning
- Interpersonal/Emotional
- Health/Fitness
- Work/Professional
- Family/Personal Relationships

Consider each of these and rate them on a scale of 1-10. (1 is most lacking; 10 is most full)

For example, on a scale of 1-10, how would you rate your current **geographic environment**? That's the current physical geographic area in which you live. Is it giving you the support you need?

What does it give you that you like? What is it missing that you might need?

This is a good opportunity to *get clear on what you want* in that aspect of your environment.

If you're not sure, do the Prioritizing Grid exercise to list all the important elements in any specific environment. Remember, you can use this grid to prioritize almost anything.

Think through the other types of environments. Are they giving you what you need? (e.g., stimulation, replenishment, etc.) For example, look at your environment related to **health/fitness**. How conducive is it to your personal health/fitness?

Feel free to use the sample environments I've listed or come up with your own.

Like me, you may want to shift certain environments at different times to get more of what you need. For example, instead of doing independent study and learning online in my field, I started attending live events. I knew I needed the camaraderie and energy of learning in person in a group setting.

PEOPLE and ENVIRONMENT Combined:

The people you surround yourself with and the environment(s) in which you live form a foundation of support for you. You can stand on that foundation when you need strength, and it can cushion you when you fall. You can bounce up from it or turn to it to get what you want out of your life and work. This foundation supports you in all aspects.

Without enough support in place, it's difficult to focus on any of three main areas discussed. Your vision could fade, your mindset might suffer, and you would have no energy to take action.

In what areas do you need more support, given where you are now?

_____

_____

_____

_____

_____

_____

_____

_____

_____

_____

_____

_____

_____

_____

_____

_____

What could be possible for you if you had all the support you need in all the areas that are important to you?

I'll answer that for you: *"Anything!"*

STORIES EXERCISE

LOOK BACK TO GET AHEAD – What's YOUR story?

The Life Work Planning process requires looking back—enough to get clues about experiences you've had that have been extremely positive, fulfilling, or rewarding. You can learn a lot by figuring out what has made those experiences stand out.

A technique detailed in *What Color Is Your Parachute?* is the **Seven Stories Exercise**. It involves recalling stories from your past that give you clues about what you do especially well, specific skills you enjoy using, and how you engage with people or things.

What seven stories stand out in your experience?

You might even give them a title. One of my stories I called "Throwing a Surprise Birthday Party." I loved throwing surprise birthday parties for my sister when we were little. Because I did it every year, people were surprised when I *stopped* doing them.

For years, I invited my sister's friends over so we could prepare a custom presentation usually in the form of a song, poem, or something silly. It was fun and creative. I detailed one of those experiences in my story, and it revealed a lot about what I enjoy: being creative, celebrating people, doing something that's unexpected, etc. These became clues about what's important in my life and work today.

Jot down your own stories—seven if you can—on the pages that follow.

Story #1 – Title:

_____
_____
_____
_____
_____
_____
_____
_____
_____
_____
_____
_____
_____
_____
_____
_____
_____
_____
_____
_____
_____
_____
_____
_____
_____
_____
_____
_____
_____
_____
_____

Story #2—Title:

_____
_____
_____
_____
_____
_____
_____
_____
_____
_____
_____
_____
_____
_____
_____
_____
_____
_____
_____
_____
_____
_____
_____
_____
_____
_____
_____
_____
_____
_____
_____
_____

Story #3—Title:

_____

_____

_____

_____

_____

_____

_____

_____

_____

_____

_____

_____

_____

_____

_____

_____

_____

_____

_____

_____

_____

_____

_____

_____

_____

_____

_____

_____

_____

_____

_____

_____

_____

_____

_____

_____

Story #4—Title:

_____
_____
_____
_____
_____
_____
_____
_____
_____
_____
_____
_____
_____
_____
_____
_____
_____
_____
_____
_____
_____
_____
_____
_____
_____
_____
_____
_____
_____
_____
_____
_____

Story #5—Title:

_____

_____

_____

_____

_____

_____

_____

_____

_____

_____

_____

_____

_____

_____

_____

_____

_____

_____

_____

_____

_____

_____

_____

_____

_____

_____

_____

_____

_____

_____

_____

_____

_____

_____

_____

Story #6—Title:

_____

_____

_____

_____

_____

_____

_____

_____

_____

_____

_____

_____

_____

_____

_____

_____

_____

_____

_____

_____

_____

_____

_____

_____

_____

_____

_____

_____

_____

_____

_____

_____

Story #7—Title:

_____

_____

_____

_____

_____

_____

_____

_____

_____

_____

_____

_____

_____

_____

_____

_____

_____

_____

_____

_____

_____

_____

_____

_____

_____

_____

_____

_____

_____

_____

_____

_____

_____

Now that you've completed your stories, look for key themes, ideas, or patterns that emerge from them. Make a note of the top skills or qualities that show up in your stories. List 10 randomly.

Use the Prioritizing Grid that follows to identify skills or qualities that go at the top of your list.

PRIORITIZING EXERCISE

What's most important?

When I ask this classic coaching question, the usual response I get is, "What's most important about what?"

That's where YOU get to set the context. There are many possibilities to consider. For example, you might ask yourself:

"What's most important to me now?" or

"What's most important in my life?" or

"What's most important to my family?" or

"What's most important to my business?"

There are no wrong answers. That question is valuable because it forces you to get clear.

For help thinking through your response, turn to the **Prioritizing Grid.** It's an analytical tool (developed by Richard Bolles) that helps you prioritize just about anything.

Take the list of the top skills you noted previously and record them in the **Prioritizing Grid.**

Follow the instructions as you work through the **Grid** to determine your top skills—ideally those you enjoy using and are good at. Pay special attention to them. Use them more deliberately in the future.

PRIORITIZING GRID

Prioritizing Grid for 10 Items

Whenever you have ten items (or less) where you need to decide which one is most important to you, which one is next most important, etc. this prioritizing grid should help immensely. Instead of trying to decide between ten items, you need only decide between two items at a time. The question is always: "If I could have *a* in my life or *b*, or *b* but not *a*, which one would I choose?"

There are four steps. **First**, just list the items you need to decide between, in any order whatsoever (this is Section A),

Secondly, compare two items at a time, using the grid in Section B. It is best to go down the grid *diagonally* (e.g.,1,2; 2,3; 3,4; 4,5; etc.) in order to avoid "knee-jerk reactions" to choosing the same number several times in a row, as often happens when you go down the grid vertically.

The **third** step is to total the number of times each item/number got circled; and then do the final ranking based on that — the item/number with the most circles has a final rank of #1, the item/number which was next most circled has a final rank of #2, etc. — all of this in Section C.

The **fourth** and final step is to copy the list all over again, this in Section D, putting the item you gave a final rank of #1 (in Section C) as your item 1 in Section D — but write out the name of the item, fully. Then look in Section C to see which has final rank #2 and copy it as 2 in section D, etc., until you have written out your whole list — now in exact order of preference.

Source: *What Color is Your Parachute?*, by Richard N. Boles. (Ten Speed Press, publishers).

Section D
After Prioritizing—
Items in final order

Section A
Before Prioritizing—
Items in any order

Section B

Section C

	1	2	3	4	5	6	7	8	9	10	
											Item number
											How many times circled
											Final rank

WorkMatters, Inc.
205.879.8494   workmatters.com

51

FINAL THOUGHTS

You are on the right path, always.

Wherever you are is exactly where you need to be. Your experiences and relationships have brought you there.

The highs and lows you've experienced have helped you gain more clarity about what you do or don't want.

Your awareness of what you do or don't want has increased so you can take your next steps with more confidence than ever.

Finding vs. creating

When you were new in the world of work, someone probably asked you, "Have you found a job?" "Have you found a place to live?" "Have you found love?" "Have you found what you're looking for?"

When you look up definitions for each word, you'll see that

a) *Find* implies discovery of something.
b) *Create* implies bringing something into being.

I encourage you to think more deliberately about *creating* (even if you don't consider yourself a creative person). Not that *finding* is necessarily a bad thing. After all, you may have had good discoveries over time. But "finding something" means discovering something you don't already have.

"Creating something" gives you more power and flexibility to make things happen in the way you want.

You come from a place of resourcefulness.

In best-case scenarios, you can create something that's even better than anything you might find.

In my own business, I didn't find the exact role models or business models I wanted to emulate, so I created my own. But you don't have to be an entrepreneur to create your own role. (If you think you do, then revisit your beliefs.)

Remember this: You can create what you want as long as you don't talk yourself (or think yourself) out of it.

Your biggest enemy

It's easy to blame other people or circumstances when you don't get what you want. But the real enemy is *you*—your own mind—when it's working against you.

I've seen too many people talk themselves out of possibilities before they give them space to grow.

It happens when you're hard on yourself. You made the presentation, but then you're beating yourself up after your talk. You constantly look around and compare yourself to others. You're worried that you're not ready for that promotion. You may even feel like an imposter in your own role.

Sometimes you might find yourself starting thoughts with, "If only . . . "

Stop it.

It doesn't matter what other people think. It matters only what *you* think.

It's your life. Now is the time to get clear and go for what you *really* want.

You can do it!

> *It's never too late to be what you might have been. ~ George Eliot*

Trust that whatever is next for you is just what it needs to be and that you will navigate (or create) turning points as you need to.

The shortest path between two points is a straight line, but this life and work journey is never straight. The process may seem slower or more difficult than you want, but with the right support and deliberate thinking, you'll move forward with more energy and purpose.

You'll be able to adjust your sail as the winds shift—or as you do.

Simply creating time and space to think differently, to question and dream, will help you begin moving toward what you want—especially compared to other people who are "too busy."

I hope your experience with this Life Work Planning Workbook has ignited new ideas and insights to help you be your best self and determine what's next for you. I'd love to hear about it.

If I can help or if interested in attending one of my Life Work Planning Retreats, please feel free to contact me by visiting WorkMatters.com

The Future

The Future is not a result of choices among alternative paths offered by the present,

But a place that is created—

Created first in mind and will,

Created next in activity.

The Future is not some place we are going,

But one we are creating.

The paths are not to be found, but made.

And the activity of making them,

changes both the maker

and the destination.

John H. Schaar

55

OTHER WORKS, RESOURCES & PROGRAMS

By Gayle Lantz

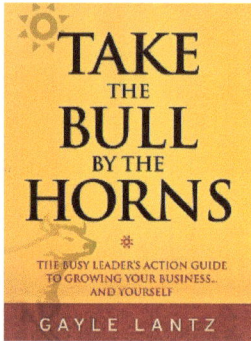

TAKE THE BULL BY THE HORNS
THE BUSY LEADER'S ACTION GUIDE TO GROWING YOUR BUSINESS... AND YOURSELF

GAYLE LANTZ

THE LEADERSHIP JOURNAL
LIFT UP. MOVE FORWARD. INSPIRE CHANGE.

Gayle Lantz

HOW TO RUN A PRODUCTIVE COMPANY RETREAT
A GUIDE FOR EXECUTIVES WHO WANT INSIGHTS ABOUT OFF-SITES

WorkMatters

Available on Kindle

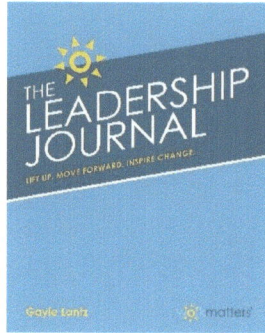

Available at Amazon.com

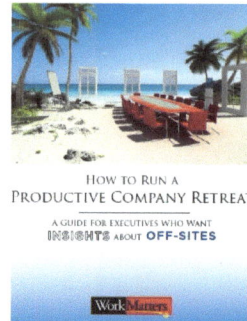

Special Report

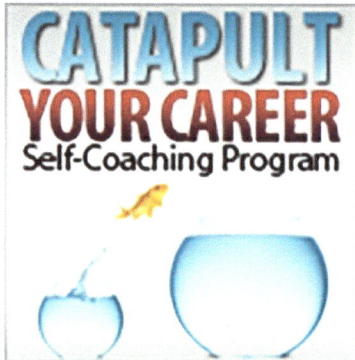

CATAPULT YOUR CAREER
Self-Coaching Program

MY DAILY COACH
BY GAYLE LANTZ
WorkMatters.com

workmatters
ACTION GUIDE
Your Guide to Leadership Growth
GAYLE LANTZ

For professionals who want to take charge of their career.

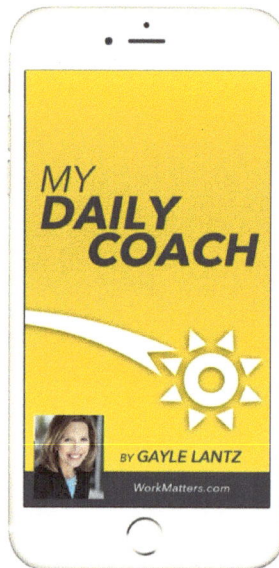

All Available at WorkMatters.com

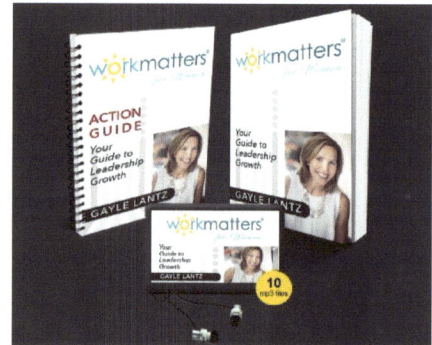

Special Online Program for Women Leaders

Notes:

_____
_____
_____
_____
_____
_____
_____
_____
_____
_____
_____
_____
_____
_____
_____
_____
_____
_____
_____
_____
_____
_____
_____
_____
_____
_____
_____
_____
_____
_____
_____
_____

Notes (continued):

Notes (continued):

Notes (continued):

_____

_____

_____

_____

_____

_____

_____

_____

_____

_____

_____

_____

_____

_____

_____

_____

_____

_____

_____

_____

_____

_____

_____

_____

_____

_____

_____

_____

_____

_____

_____

_____

_____

_____

www.ingramcontent.com/pod-product-compliance
Lightning Source LLC
Chambersburg PA
CBHW061056090426
42742CB00002B/59